Here, There, and Everywhere

Here, There, and Everywhere

Redmond Association of Spokenword Poetry Anthology

Michael Dylan Welch, Editor

Redmond Association of Spokenword
Redmond, Washington

Redmond Association of Spokenword
Redmond, Washington

Here, There, and Everywhere

Michael Dylan Welch, Editor

Laura Lee Bennett, Assistant Editor
Elizabeth Carroll Hayden, Assistant Editor

ISBN 978-1-4921-5198-2
First printing, August 2013
Revised September 2013

Design, typography, and cover photograph by Michael Dylan Welch.
Poems and names set in 12/15 Garamond Premier Pro
with headings set in 15/18 Gill Sans Bold.

www.raspread.com

Contents

Introduction

"To have great poets there must be great audiences too."
—Walt Whitman

Virginia Woolf spoke of having a room of one's own in which to write. Writers of all kinds know that they also benefit from having a community in which to thrive—an extended family where they can share and test their writing ideas. Without an attentive audience, trusted feedback, and a dash of praise, that room of one's own can potentially become a prison rather than a sanctuary. But with the right community, the writer can indeed flourish.

The Redmond Association of Spokenword, also known as RASP, provides an energetic community and sense of belonging to writers in and around the city of Redmond, Washington. It expands the sanctuary of the writer's lonely garrison, encompassing fiction, non-fiction, and poetry. While this anthology honors poetry, it is part of a larger context in the RASP community—a full range of writing by the group's talented participants.

In the years since RASP was founded in 1997, the organization has had many accomplishments. It is my hope that this book contributes to the group's successes, but also celebrates the accomplishments of its individual contributors. The poets whose work you'll read here include new contributors and longtime RASP regulars, as well as many of the best-known poets of the Seattle area who have been guest poets at our monthly readings—for which I have served as curator since 2008. The interactions of all these poets enlarge not only our community but influence the broader poetry community of the entire Seattle area and beyond.

The heart of each RASP meeting is its open-mic reading. That's where RASP's experienced and first-time participants find a platform to share their work. And it's where many first-timers have *become* experienced. Reading work aloud to an attentive audience helps each poet refine his or her performance, while the audience hones its listening skills. Together, careful reading and listening has helped to build a strong and supportive community.

The poems in this anthology—120 poems by 70 poets—have naturally fallen into three groupings. The first section, "Here," encompasses 22 poems about the Pacific Northwest, and sometimes more specifically the here and now of poetry readings—perhaps even of RASP itself. The second section, "There," gathers 28 poems that point to geographical locations farther afield. The third section, "Everywhere," with 70 poems, is not just a catch-all for the remaining poems but a celebration of the range of diversity present in the RASP community and the many styles of its poetry. The assignment of poems to particular sections may be subjective, but I trust that you will find some aspect of the sectional theme in each of that section's poems—and also enjoy each poem on its own terms. Together, I hope these three sections take you on a rewarding trip—here, there, and everywhere. Thank you for reading.

Michael Dylan Welch, Editor

Acknowledgments

Many hands contributed to this anthology. Michael Dylan Welch first proposed the project, and the entire board of the Redmond Association of Spokenword refined the details of his proposal. This included setting a length limit of thirty lines, the practicality of which precluded longer work that would more accurately represent the range of our contributors. RASP president Michael Heavener initially publicized this project through the group's website and mailing list. He had extensive help from Laura Lee Bennett and Elizabeth Carroll Hayden who contacted key participants of the Redmond Association of Spokenword, past and present, including featured poets at our many monthly readings. Assistant editors Laura Lee and Liz then worked long hours to receive and compile the submissions. Except for a number of last-minute submissions, all poems were scored anonymously by a team of reviewers, using a scoring rubric developed chiefly by Laura Lee and Liz. Michael Dylan Welch also read all submissions anonymously and then made final selections after comparing his preferences with the average scores and comments of the review team. The team's scores frequently pushed selections in one direction or another, but all final selections were Michael's, who sought to be as inclusive as possible. Many thanks to the review team, which consisted of Rebecca Meredith, Allison Ohlinger, Heidi Stahl, and Vonnie Thompson (who did not score their own poems), and to RASP board members not already named: Pamela Denchfield, Bill Hayes, and Mike Meredith. And thanks again to Laura Lee and Liz for going above and beyond by tightening many of this book's nuts and bolts. They did a stellar job of pulling everything together from here, there, and everywhere. But above all, thank you to the ever-surprising and talented RASP community for offering its poems for consideration and for supporting this lively literary arts organization through thick and thin for sixteen years.

Here

Leaving the Island

ferry from Orcas to Anacortes

Mist-colored knots of sea glass. A moss-clot
cadged from the trail's edge. The truce

fished word by word from beneath the surface,
still unspoken. We carry what we found

what we made there. Three days you and I
let the currents direct our course, slept

on cool sand, let woodsmoke flavor us.
What's left? Slow travel over cold water.

Toward home and days ordered by clocks
instead of tides. We watch through salt-scarred

windows, hoping the dark shapes will rise
beside us, will grace us. We know too well

what can't be willed, only missed
if we look away too soon.

Elizabeth Austen
Seattle, Washington

Summer Solstice Riff to America
from Point Hudson Jetty

Sometimes the pack of yellow dogs you see is not coyote,
merely a trio of black-tailed deer marooned in pale light.

Gaunt one looks me in the eye, hesitates, then scavenges
low tide scrabble kelp, tattered magenta, while two does
stand aloof, in the margins of a dream.

Aloft, fake hollow owls perch mizzenmasts of yawls
moored in the cove, rigged for Glacier Bay, the Bering Sea,
the deep, measured in fathoms, orange survival suits.

Even local cormorants hitchhike dinghies towed by beamy
oak ketches, the Cascade mountain chain, scissor-cut,
like the first time we sail the Sound, close-haul, starboard tack,

squall beating down our coordinates, salt air frizzled like splayed
rind of tangerine, and the pomegranate
for Rosh Hashanah, my friend, Wendy, gave to me,

meaning, *precious the New Year*—bitter seed to stain the tongue,
plum pink, like the hue of the emissions plume
over the cardboard box factory, south of town, like the tint

of diesel fumes from the Foss tug as she putt-putts the Strait,
Anacortes-bound—the otter by the pier, pewter in morn's
first glint—see her?—carbon dioxide exhalation rising, quicksilver,

to the chime of the halyard cleat, bleat of the buoy bell—the Bay
a vat of crimson; and East, backlit wings of doves.

Denise Calvetti Michaels
Kirkland, Washington

Cove

Bay-crossing ferry disappears behind the cove
As scarlet-salmon twilight darkens into mauve.
Horizon opal glows through, blends with cedar grove
As still and silent as maroon-black peak
Below that wispy saffron cirrus streak.
Now, tired can feel good. I risked, I learned, I strove.

David D. Horowitz
Seattle, Washington

Boat Dreams

Dry-docked on a backyard lawn, the boat
endures
rust and rotting wood.
In her dreams she
rocks and sways, remembering—
pride of new paint,
tread of feet, creak of oars,
tug of wind and slap of sail,
smell of fresh-caught fish: and most of all,
the lift and lap
of water.

Marie Helen Turner
Playa Vista, California

What's Happened So Far

My turn came, I was given a wooden board.
Our boards were different lengths—the distribution
random. A man and woman escorted me to the ship's railing.
They hoisted me up, set me walking out
over the ocean. On calm days I found it easy to balance,
to venture far. The sea birds flew overhead
black eyes watching my progress. I misunderstood,
detecting some sense of safety in their presence,
as though they could pluck me up mid-fall.
But they're just small, winged creatures with hollow bones,
not even curious at the expression
on my face before hitting the water.
Eventually my board bent. What appeared to be solid fir
was filled with knots and little cracks. The seas began building,
the ship pitched harder and harder, I looked up
this time noticing the arc of the birds' wings
and I leapt to join them.

Erin Fristad
Port Townsend, Washington

Sap

The wind's
familiar hand
through my
April hair.
Sand and salt
creep into my nose,
lungs—I beg
the smells to remain
until next spring.
Overhead
confident clouds
collide, merge as one
continuous mass.
Ocean's fog
veils me then
succumbs to sun break.
I dream
of tapping sap.
It drips into
my small metal cup.
I rush home,
boil it, add sugar.
I drain it
over waffles,
catching each
drop
as if it were
my life.

Janée J. Baugher
Seattle, Washington

Jelly

Jellyfish
Are perfectly horrid.
They're balls of mindless hunger,
shooting little harpoons into tasty guppies, inedible kelp
and the bare knees of children too slow or ignorant
to avoid the little mermaid manes of these scourges.
So watching a horde of them die
glowing their last in a phosphorescent low tide was satisfying.
Or at least it was until my girlfriend waded into the receding ocean.
She scooped the harmless blue jellies up in her soft white hands
and deposited them one quivering mass at a time into deeper brine.
Reeking algae stuck to her shapely, fresh-shaved legs
and rough particles of sand clung to her dainty toes.
I touched one of the jellies with the very edge of a cautious fingernail.
The creature acknowledged me with the weak light of primitive nerves.
Squeamish, I left him to fate and the pull of a careless moon.

S. A. Upton
Redmond, Washington

Labor Day Weekend, Along the Hood Canal

On this trip to Seal Rock Campground, we stop,
eat Quilcene oysters,
and squirt fresh-cut lemons
we buy from teens in the shucking factory,
south of here, on Highway 101.

We sit on cedar
graffitied with the names
of other lovers who've made promises
on scent of saltwater, spill of Milky Way.

No children skip the beach path barefoot,
gather agates
and silver madrona slivers at the high-water mark.

Fifteen years ago you work weekends.
I ferry the girls
Seattle to the Peninsula,
load the blue Buick we buy for fifty dollars
with the mail-order tent I stitch on the Singer,
a camping family, last baby under a year

before I know oysters can teach me
where to place the knife,
how to pry the hinge,
and lift the cover of a thimble-size sea.

We eat them raw on the beach,
so the throb at the center, returns,
a knot, a cry.

Denise Calvetti Michaels
Kirkland, Washington

On the Cliff Between Far and Near East Beaches

Indralaya, Orcas Island

Where does this wind come from?

Did it caress the bell
in the white steeple?

This wind—
kissing my face at 2:30 this afternoon—
who did it kiss at 9:15 this morning?

My downward thoughts,
carried away
Do they break up—
Disperse—
like sea foam?

Do they reincarnate
ten years from now
as white fawn lilies
on some unseen hillside?

Who is writing this poem?

The wind?

The eagle whose shadow
just passed over my face?

H. R. Stahl
Redmond, Washington

This

It's cold on this Memorial Day;
a boy in a swimsuit trudges up
the beach on the riverbank
and instructs his family to move
to Florida. Baby sister
kneels by the water and wails
for half an hour, while their father
sits on his ass and barks orders.
A pack of jet skis rattles past,
organic and mechanical whining
entwining like sonic barbed wire.

I finish my reading and leave,
just as a woman arrives with her daughter,
who looks barely three. Watching her toes
sink into the sand, the girl announces
"This is fun," like Adam announcing
"This is an aardvark." A few feet on,
she says it again, as if to assure us
this matter has now been settled.

Dennis Caswell
Woodinville, Washington

Letter Thirteen—Plum Stain

Poetry found in the sky
like giant Mars chasing the full ripe plum moon as if in
love—interstellar courting
is how bodies in the heavens demonstrate—
made gravity desirable again
in the August night sky   above the Honda's pounding bass
a silent witness   above the
bed in which dreams of hook shots & fast breaks are kept.

In the Slaughter sky
her makeup perfect   this ripe plum full moon   fallen plums
messed
up sidewalks all over town
sheets of falling unwanted fruit
the Russians learn about the Slaughter
sun
rises   plums fall & Mars ran away w/ the moon.

Poetry—the desire to kiss eternity
lives to leave a ripe plum stain on the sidewalk of the future
in Slaughter   where the
deep wounds open   but don't reveal flesh   deep
woods open   reinvent themselves in an alder moment   to show Slaughter
the way.

6:37AM – 8.13.03
(Phrase taken from Andre Breton—On the Road to San Romano)

Paul E. Nelson
Seattle, Washington

On Poetry and Other Irritants

Honestly, what's the point?
If you have to say something,
Say it, don't marinade it in saucy words and chop
Up your phrases like
Sad radishes.

You poets annoy me, always
Have to be so clever.
No one understands what you are saying.
No one cares.

What's to be written that's more important than
Bus Stop
Exit
Mini Mart
Donuts?

I can look at clouds as well as you can,
Conch shells,
Tree sap,
Whippoorwill—
All of that.
So?

Just stop it—
Your peering at light and shadow
Your hanging backwards over stone benches
Your listening for when dusk becomes twilight.
You write
As if you're going to die.

Katherine Grace Bond
Mill Creek, Washington

Exhortation

Poets! You are the lips on fish swimming the upstream
of tomorrow, the fish resurrected after the ocean succumbs
to the tongue of dead economies, dead ideologies,
the moribund and liquefying rhetoric of the hedge fund.
Poets! You are the tango of redemption, the cha-cha
of chutzpah, the Aztec two-step of the be-bop of ecology.
You are the ace up the sleeve of the laughing Buddha,
the codex of afternoon sex, the ex-stutterer texting
the elocution experts, the voice of Nav saying
turn left at the next chromosomal mutation, right on
the sublimated passion parkway, straight into the womb of
yes. Poets! Ask not what your askew sanity can juice
from the reproductive machinery of death, but what the
caliginous junk heap of death says of the living.
Poets! Eschew the static of deception
that pits us versus our verses, me versus you,
red versus blue, mind versus heart. Poets!
Let your words be a start, a seed, a lantern
in nightest dark, let them illuminate the pumpkin's
grin, the fugue of longing in a dog's meow,
the sperm romancing the egg, the ancient chant
streaming from compassion to regeneration
to muse to music to the polyphonic squeal
of gladness fruiting again and again in the
hotchpotch stewpot of fecund life. Poets!

Michael Schein
Carnation, Washington

If I Ever Mistake You for a Poem

No body was ever composed
from words, not the hipsway

of verse, the iambic beat of a heart.
Yet inside you, a sestina
of arteries, the villanelle of villi,
sonnets between your shoulder blades.

If I were more obsessive I'd follow
the alliteration of age spots across

your arms. But I have exchanged
my microscope for a stethoscope

as I want to listen inside you, past
your repetition, your free verse of skin.
How easy it is to fall for your internal
organs. Your arrhythmia is charming
hidden in the ballad of body,
your gurgling stanzas, your lyric sigh.

Kelli Russell Agodon
Kingston, Washington

Tiger Trick

So a magician, a mentalist, and a poet walk into a bar. Always the same questions when the other patrons learn their trades: *Do you know how they do that tiger trick in Vegas—Have you ever met The Amazing Kreskin—What kind of poetry do you write?* The magician is reading about the physiology of Houdini's lungs. *Do you know—*he nudges the poet—*that Ginsberg guy had quite a pair too. Practiced reciting his lines face down in the bathtub. No shit—in the tub!* Meanwhile, the mentalist orders drinks telepathically and realizes how tired he has grown of bending spoons and always knowing the punch line. In fact all three are bored with the particular way they exploit the malleable. The magician sometimes wishes he were lyric, but he gets such great results with *voilà! presto, change-o!* and *hocus-pocus.* And the poet, yes, the poet—he keeps trying to saw his words in half, dreams about pulling a sestina out of his hat.

Marjorie Manwaring
Seattle, Washington

For the Crime of Poetry

If they are looking through my trash
They'll know I'm a poet
And that I like microwave pizza
If they take me in and torture me
I'll have a brave face for a moment
But then give all of you up
All the names I remember
And I'm so bad with names
I'll probably make some up
They'll be smoking outside the open-mics
Dressed to look like bikers or malcontents
They'll wait for each of you to get up
Recording all the evidence they need
They'll come in all officious yells and swagger
They'll catch you running out the backdoor
Jumping through the window
Hiding in the women's bathroom
We'll go on hunger strikes
We'll petition an unsympathetic state
We'll stand under the waving stars and stripes
And be shot against concrete walls
Our families will wail
Then be quiet
Because we are traitors
They'll get the novelists next

Shane Guthrie
Duvall, Washington

The Beer Ted Kooser Owes Us All

"Twenty-four hours in a day, twenty-four beers in a case. Coincidence? I think not." —H. L. Menken

I go to Safeway
to buy a six-pack.
Somebody's taken
a bottle from the
last pack, so now it's

a fiver, dammit.
Was it Kooser?—that
geezer (my mom finds
cute) who wrote about
the miracle of

a lone beer bottle
standing right side up
and empty along
the highway—each line
three syllables long,

each stanza three lines.
My students read this
without awe, as though
they've done this plenty
after polishing

off a bottle at
fifty, cruising down
Aurora, tossing
emptiness to wind.

Jared Leising
Seattle, Washington

Small Talk

Akira Kurosawa does not wish to discuss the weather.
He is only interested in his next film.

I was standing on a street corner in Seattle, waiting for the walk sign. A man wearing a three-piece-suit and designer glasses asked if I knew whether the Dow Jones Industrials had closed up or down. I immediately ran out into traffic.

Akira Kurosawa does not wish to discuss the weather.

Small talk is like Einstein's special theory. Topics of conversation are either red shifting or blue shifting. One has to wonder which is more interesting, fission or fusion? Traveling near the speed of light alters one's perception of time as does participating in idle chit-chat at a cocktail party.

Akira Kurosawa does not wish to discuss the weather.

When a hard-bitten custodian on my crew tells me about his gambling exploits at Spirit Mountain Casino, I feign interest and secretly wish I was reading the William S. Burroughs novel *The Ticket That Exploded*. When I tell a hard-bitten custodian on my crew that I am reading the William S. Burroughs novel *The Ticket That Exploded*, he feigns interest and secretly wishes he was gambling at Spirit Mountain Casino.

Akira Kurosawa does not wish to discuss the weather.

In a tavern that still sells stubbies of Olympia a man tells me how great it is for the Portland Trailblazers that they acquired Scottie Pippen from the Chicago Bulls. I look him straight in the eye and say, "My doctor forgot to lubricate her glove before my last prostate exam."

Akira Kurosawa is only interested in his next film.

Kevin Mooneyham
Eugene, Oregon

Lantern Floating Ceremony

Green Lake, Seattle, August 6, 2005

Like water falling
over smooth, slick rock
thirsty souls beg
for peace, justice, wisdom.

This is our cry

Taiko drums echo
the cries of 60 years ago.
Voices sing, "Peace like a river
in my soul."

This is our prayer

Hiroshima is my shame.
Sand Creek is my history.
Rwanda is my horror.

Bring peace to the world

Slowly, silently people walk
to the shore, lanterns lit
floating messages of peace.

The water is witness.

Linda Thompson
Kenmore, Washington

Lake Washington

Tonight we are quiet
Huddled on this stony beach
Watching lake-flow. Cold winding channels
Reflect grey sky in twilight blue.
Moody breezes ripple the surface and
Concrete bridges the depths.
Edges are pierced by pilings, boat sheds.

This is how love changes when fear questions
The heart. Days spill over with smiles half meant
While chilly replies wind through the hours.
Nights are darkened by deeper fears—
Channels of sadness moving there.

So we sit patiently, comforted for a time
By more natural rhythms. The hushing sound
Of small waves on stone fill the silence
But not the wounds
As we consider
The lengthening shadows.

ChiChi Stewart
Kirkland, Washington

Seattle Summer Sonnet

Shall I compare thee to a summer's day?
Thou art less transient and less o'ercast;
Chill rains do soak the mossy growth of May,
And August's warmth has seldom proved to last;

This northwest sky presents a face so blue
That hearts are torn asunder by her face;
Her fickle winds to reason's course won't hew,
Though wizards would their winding path fain trace.

But all of summer's brightness quickly'd fade
Did thee but smile, or merely quirk a grin;
And all those sweetly scented days I'd trade
To wrap a single night with thee therein.

So long as in this soggy land I be,
My port in stormy weather's found in thee.

Jason Zions
Bellevue, Washington

The Last Summer Canoeing with My Father on the Deschutes River

The river runs flat by the reedy grass
and passes by the shore. Meandering
icy water flows as high desert sun
drifts down and warms our shoulders. The gentle
suck of water, paddle sharp cuts the skin
and slices the river's yielding marrow.

The oars swoosh again, split the river's shell.
Swift streams spill off the wood and vanish deep
in the dank Deschutes wending past its banks
like those monstrous filaments that travel
through my father's lungs. He laughs, lifts his blade,
splashes the youngest. The last of summer's

      memories drape around us as we watch
      him drown in pneumonia's fetid water.

Elizabeth Carroll Hayden
Bellevue, Washington

There

The Art of Knowing

no one knows you are coming and going underneath
this big sky and drinking a hundred vowels each

minute, drinking and spitting

you are walking underneath the awning of a petite
French-style café and someone five miles away

doesn't know

Maya Ganesan
Redmond, Washington

Brown County, 1909

Trouble in the kitchen
With the skillet
Paul dug the outhouse
Too shallow this time
Got a full coop of
Chickens and children
Sure could use a whiskey
But I'm pregnant again

Monica Schley
Seattle, Washington

June 24, 1977

There is rain moving in.
I can see the storm clouds
Moving in
From the north and west, and feel
The wind coming up with
Threat and thunder.

Wet air comes,
Blowing sweet and cool
Across my cheek.
A wonder of a sky-blown river.

What's left of bright and blue
Slips down the southeast sky.
Scattered pearl-drops
Spot the porch around my feet,
And I'll have to turn the lights on
In the house
When I go back inside.

Barbara Stoner
Seattle, Washington

She Decides Not to Look Back

So. You've come all this way, colored your hair
and still the disguise doesn't stick.
The way the snakeskin slithers up your side
you'd never know your bag and boots
beg to tell another story. And mother,
is it a good one. We started in a small town,
pregnant; we started out on the road on our own;
we left behind brothers and sisters that needed us;
we wanted to see the city lights. We wanted to bring home
a father, a lover, a new name. We grew tamer by lamplight.
Tease your hair and grow talons, but your soft breath
just escapes. Remember your hometown, the accent you lost,
the school counselor who told you to give up and get married.
Remember that childhood friend who burned himself to death,
the one who fried his brain, the one who turned himself inside out.
You know you couldn't save. You have your six degrees
of separation. You were lucky you ran
when you did with just the change in your pocket.

Jeannine Hall Gailey
Redmond, Washington

Dana's Waiting Song

Back in the days of helmet laws
you were a hot white burr,
knocking those troopers to the asphalt
like a real criminal.
They never noticed you wore jockey shorts
instead of a hat.

Your "cycle broke down,"
so you hitchhiked to reach me.
Mardi Gras, Baton Rouge,
a swipe of Mississippi mud.
I didn't answer your postcards.

When I sat by the river
I could hear you piping in the reeds
Ripe calluses would press me into sleep.
I'd dream of you finally here, my dunesman,
tearing the slips and panties I hand you
for your next journey.

Laura Lee Bennett
Redmond, Washington

Permanent

Our Huckleberry Finn daffodils
split loudly into color.

In the early summer
we'd climb up on top

of the garden shed
between planting

the rhododendrons and the azaleas
and watch cars seesaw

along the farm road
then disappear.

One summer they stopped driving by,
and the road fell hard

into the hush of the grass.
I waited for the flowers

to drift away,
prize-winning perennials to slip

into mud,
but they never left home.

Maya Ganesan
Redmond, Washington

The Spaulding-Criss-Potter-Craig-Sherer-Smith-Walker Women Ponder the Corrals They've Built Inside

(1809–2012)

There was a time they roped whitepicketfences from the saddle of want.
They thought they were wrestling hiredhands, not their own barbedwire.
They believed a hotwoodstove meant shoveling loveshit from horsestall to garden.
Sometimes, they fought their own dustdevils with tobacco and candlefire
and once or twice, they drank Kentucky bourbon until the cowmen came home
(their cowchildren sponging vomit from the braided rug before anyone came home).
Othertimes, they wore his loose pants until those pants tightened like a promise,
then sweetwords rode their hearts and they finally hung up their nagspurs.
When they got older, they herded their wanderingmisgivings into a ribcagecorral.
They retell and retell stirrupstories, bridle, halter, hobble.
They retell and retell bridlestories, stirrup, halter, hobble and hayfork. And hayfork.
With ropes braided from secondhandscarves, they tie all their wildhorses
to a post, drink westwind, loosen the corsetbras that hold in their heartsalt.

Annette Spaulding-Convy
Kingston, Washington

Why She Would Take Off Her Shoes Before Jumping from the Golden Gate Bridge

Maybe the water
is a temple

and white boats below
so many devotees

pointing
where to lay down

the orchid of herself,
incense burning

like salt.
She doesn't want

to bring the road's dirt
inside,

but unbuckles on the step
and tears open

the soft door,
floating gulls screaming

like angels.

Annette Spaulding-Convy
Kingston, Washington

Long Journey

"On a long, difficult pilgrimage, Bashō wrote on his hat."
—Mike Puican, "And the Gauchos Sing"

Day five of the ten-day silent meditation retreat
I grew itchy
on my pillow in the hall
saw myself crossing the gravel parking lot
firing up the Corolla
heading south on I-5
to my sister's place in Orange County,
arriving just in time for Christmas

Following the rules, I hadn't brought a journal
not even a pen
night alone in the room
no one could see me staring at the ceiling
or pacing
but staring and pacing were not strong enough verbs
to stop the itch

Bare feet on cold, dusty wooden floor
hand on cold doorknob
breath held, easing open the door
down the hallway
into the bathroom
where hung the laminated shower sign-up sheet
and a black dry-erase pen

I snuck them back to my room
scribbled, filling the blank back side,
then erased,
then filled it up again.

H. R. Stahl
Redmond, Washington

Early Times

Spring comes down in a March wind
Flapping white sheets in my face
On a late April day north of Chicago.

Caroline in green with hair like
Dandelion silk
Sits in the new sun among
The yellow flower faces.

The sheets snap like wet towels
At my face and arms
And I laugh up into the ragged white flapping
And April blue sky.

Caroline is laughing and lifting up her arms,
Her fists full of fuzzy flower feathers.

We've been to the garden
And on a blue plate in the grass
The first radishes are red and ripe
And riposte off my tongue.

Barbara Stoner
Seattle, Washington

Clock Tower Pantoum

Austin, Texas

There are tiny green speakers in the trees on Trinity
to scare away warblers, to keep them from shitting
on sweaty conventioneers shuffling inside, where air
is conditioned and colorless cameras bleed into walls

to scare away warblers, to keep them from shooting
a keynote whose words rest in the safe of his mouth
conditioned and white, hidden beneath the camera
he's holding up to his face, pointing it at the sounds

coming from a tree, a speaker whose words wrestle
with real birds' desires to leave their chalky marks
on dark shoulders and what's on his face, pointing
feathers like Whitman's scope and rifle at passersby

with real birds' desires to leave their chalky marks
on conventioneers shuffling inside, where feathers
sever air like Whitman's bullets and buckshot because
there are tiny green speakers in the trees on Trinity.

Jared Leising
Seattle, Washington

The Longest Word

It was in the school yard of PS 89, Queens, in 1955
that I first heard the longest word of my life:
"antidisestablishmentarianism."
Ralph Hammelbacher said it fastest:
"antidisestablishmentarianism" . . .
and we each repeated it ourselves, amazed at our brilliance,
at our ability to so conquer the English language.

"Antidisestablishmentarianism"—
we whipped out the word
while sitting at the soda parlor counter,
the jukebox playing Bing Crosby singing
"Would you like to swing on a star?"
as we ate the scrumptious banana splits
Mr. Wolke concocted with homemade ice cream,
using the secret recipe he brought from Vienna after the War.
He never put his bananas in the refrigerator—
"No, no, no, no, no, no, no."
They melted, sweet and ripe,
under the vanilla-scented whipped cream.

I rolled it out again quickly, trippingly, on my tongue—
"antidisestablishmentarianism."
But it wasn't bigger than the word
we had learned the day before in science:
"Hydrogen."
That word was really scary,
because it was followed by the small word:
"bomb."

Peggy Barnett
Woodinville, Washington

It Begins to Make Sense
When You Hear the Music

I want to hear the symphony,
cacophony of instruments,
a blacksmith's rhythmic strikes upon his anvil,
a pickup practicing its cough and sputter,
on skylights, the drumming of the rain.

I want to hear the thud inside my chest
at New Year's and the Fourth when BOOM
my neighbor's cannon BOOM goes unannounced,
sets off a chain of barking dogs—
I like to hear them howl at thunder.

I want to hear the Beatles sing
"I want to hold your hand," the tenor leap
an octave up from baritone and bass.
To take me back to Central Park I turn
the juice on high for Simon and Garfunkel.

I want recorders to recall
their ancient fantasies and airs.
From players poised and set to breathe,
I want, before the first note sounds,
to hear that moment's pregnant pause.

Winifred Jaeger
Kirkland, Washington

Tornado—Iowa Acrostic

I blew into town just as Ma Yoder was slidin' the
Ore Idas and casserole out of the oven.
When she heard the storm sirens she hollers,
"Alvin, find Jesse and Nate and git down to the cellar!"

Charlene Alberhasky had just taken her long johns
        down from the line and was bringin' 'em
Inside the doublewide when she turns around
        about the time I'm spiralin' down
Towards the north forty of the Altmeier farm
        a mile north of Lone Tree. Well,
        Charlene, she quick grabs her
Yeller cat, Bootsie, and hightails out to the
        drainage ditch by the side of Route 22.

I made quick work of Ma Yoder's fine dinner.
        I rained tater tots and most of
        the family's shingles and siding
Out along Iowa Avenue all the way up to
        South Governor Street. Although poor
        Bootsie's ol' heart gave out in fright,
When you drive by the Swartzendruber farm
        house along Route 22 near Nichols
A pair of Charlene Alberhasky's heather grey
        Munsingwear long johns can still be seen
        where I left them, flappin' like a banner atop
        a battered chinkapin oak.

James Parrott
Seattle, Washington

I Didn't Miss the Robins

till we were here down the Cape last weekend
and there they were again
on the grassy banks that line the highway;
on lawns, resolute among the blowing leaves,
intent on sound beneath the surface;
thronging the branches of small trees
with yellowed leaves and bright red berries
where they arrive singly
but always seem to depart
in furious one-on-one pursuit,
a feeding and mating frenzy like—
well, a lot like *summer* on the Cape.

The first robin of spring
is like the clicking of a tumbler
in some marvelously complex lock,
a milestone like a birthday,
the longest day of the year,
the first time I told my father
that I loved him.

But there's never anything about
the last robin of fall
that announces it
as last.

Jack McCarthy
Seattle, Washington

Homecoming

(Triangle factory fire of 1911)

As much explosion as a fire, most
were dead in minutes. Flames spread so fast
that sixty jumped like skydivers spilling
from the windows. Their skirts and petticoats,
unlike parachutes to land them softly,
streamed and never caught the air to billow.

The wounded were attended to, the shocked
were left to wander home or gratefully
accept the help of strangers, telling us
a nice man took us home . . . or, *. . . gave us carfare . . .*
or, *. . . let me wear his coat,* and Rose, God knows,
met her girlfriend after work to shop.

They should have been in sunlight in the park,
laughing, flirting, but they worked six days
a week and gave their pay to help support
their families who held them tightly. Mobs
and murder, pogroms not forgotten, fear
ingrained into parent's lives, persisted.

In turn, their daughters were afraid the news
might throw them into panic. One escaped
the hospital, because her mother was sick.
My God, one said, *I hope they don't find out.*
Not everyone was welcomed home. Until
the truth was known, some were treated harshly.

Donald Kentop
Seattle, Washington

Size

What she thought was large—a 64-ounce Big Gulp,
boxcars creaking from one end of town to the other,

Jupiter's red spot, the silvery, sweeping pinwheel galaxy—
are tinier than the tiniest bone in a pygmy shrew.

Big, it turns out, is 300,000 light-years wide,
a dark corona surrounding the Milky Way,

which it wears like the halo of an angel
in mourning, a cloud-like penumbra, a gypsy's

funereal kerchief ten times the size of every visible star,
every trace of dust, gasp of gas, each planetary speck.

Try that on for size. Try on the black *babushka*
beyond which everything else is shroud-less mycoplasma.

This is the size of her thoughts as she walks down row after row
at the Tomb of the Unknowns, lowers her small and uncloaked head.

Martha Silano
Seattle, Washington

She's Building a Model of Falling Water

She's building a model of Falling Water,
Cantilevered concrete slabs of gingerbread and fondant
Propped up by some I-beams carved from home-made candy canes
And anchored by cement of royal frosting.

The roof can be removed, exposing
Stickley furniture of marshmallow and cookies
Occupied by people made of sugar lace and food-safe dye
And sheer bravado.

Last week she did a rendering of
Gaudi's great Sagrada Familia as it
Rises over Barcelona, outer facets
Bas relief in sugar and molasses, hyperbolic sectioned
Plinths and corbels carved from halvah
Perched on columns formed of laminated honeyed phyllo dough
And firm expectance.

Every year is much the same; she
Builds these little homes for God and man of
Edible ephemera, of waking dreams and fairy dust,
And steely whim.

Jason Zions
Bellevue, Washington

Dorothy Does Italy

Once bitten, the travel bug stayed with her,
and she traded gusting dust storms
for jet streams and skipped the stratosphere
to emeraldine cities across the globe.
Right now she's in Venice (not the one in Nebraska)
discovering the putrid pungency of canals omitted by
those travel brochures' four-color pitch for romance.
Always there's a catch,
she thinks, *the stinker behind the curtain.*

Even so she considers the gondolas graceful and imagines
a postcard of courageous Toto (long dead, buried) riding head high
at the heel of a boat, barking for joy into the witchy fog.
Jolted from her reverie by a timid waiter with tin-blue eyes,
she nods yes for another espresso and wonders if tonight's the night
her ruby dancing shoes will raise one hell of a memorable gale.

Lana Hechtman Ayers
Kingston, Washington

Old Woman Dying

In a straw hat and white Spanish sundress,
she tends to the sunflowers—
their yellow extensions press out, reaching.

Through the veranda, the French doors
open to the kitchen where Chopin plays.
She steeps oolong tea and arranges currant scones

(middled with homemade preserves) on earthenware.
In bare feet she walks out across the terra cotta patio.
She sets down the tray and removes the Indian corn

centerpiece from the wicker table. She settles back,
scans her patchwork-pattern garden: the carrots,
potatoes, dill. A wall of string cheers beans to climb.

Each dogwood dangles a birdfeeder.
A path of fresh bark divides the shaggy lawn.
Petunias bloom pastels. Irises,

proud blue violet with that slight stroke of sun.
Draped in expectant grape vines, the bower shades her.
The old tabby sleeps in the chair next to her.

She jots down words, sips tea
and catches pastry crumbs in her lap.

Janée J. Baugher
Seattle, Washington

The Widows

Down in Kosciusko, the widow women
hire black men to come out and cut the yard,
and white men to come in and fix the sink.
They smoke cigarettes at twilight on the porch,
another lightning bug amid the closed day lilies.
Inside, the pendulum clocks strike
from walls filled with men's smiling faces
at weddings, graduations, family reunions—
a roll call of the departed, and the simply gone.
And even though they aren't there any more
to take up the lunch box and go to the school bus factory
or out to the tractors and the herds,
their women's gnarled feet slide into the scuffs at 5 a.m.
And they light the first one of the day,
put the coffee and the weather channel on,
look around them and sigh, thinking
they have finally got everything fixed just the way they want it,
and tomorrow will be soon enough
to go out and check the flowers on the Old Man's grave.

Rebecca Meredith
Seattle, Washington

Orkney Equinox

In Orkney
where millennia swell
from the sward,
lapwings lift,
dense as beeswarm,
hang from the low sky,
wheel,
restless for a Summerland.
The gales come in, they say,
at equinox,
dividing harvest,
bonniest time of
the year.
And, capping the wind,
cloud so persistent
tints and hues shift there,
pale borealis
in carded wool vapor.
In Stromness,
behind the old kirk,
a clutch of trees,
bent with birds:
their autumn vespers
brim the tangled
streets into dusk.
Only weeks now until cows
are stone-byred against
long-toothed winter,
baying into the bitter night.

Beth Atwood
Redmond, Washington

Goldsworthy

(British artist, born 1959)

Stacker of stone, sculptor
of ice carved into blocks
yet translucent. Mound
builder of earth made
serpentine and undulant
through woods, architect
of seaside bamboo spires,
the tide giveth, the tide
taketh away. Fabricator
of slate circles, spirals
formed of leaf and twig,
hands raw with cold,
craggy as Northern wind.
A solitary sage content
with birds for company,
who saw in autumn elms
a red wound in green forests,
whose leaves he gave to a
river unwinding in its flow
like a salmon-bellied sunset sky
waiting for the moon to rise.

William Scott Galasso
Edmonds, Washington

The muse has the right to know
About the nonstop stream of consciousness
Of men with incomplete Ph.D.s
Recovering from the existential damage of higher education
In the elite corner of a street coffee shop, downtown Cairo
Surrounded by stray dogs
And the disintegrated institutions
Of a State that had collapsed thousands of years ago
In order to offer them the necessary reasons
To explore the gaps of their sexual longing
And the world that is being—pointlessly—longed for

Maged Zaher
Seattle, Washington

Reading with Alzheimer's

Sprawled out
in the recliner
wearing
a tie-dyed shirt
the kids
gave him,
a Middle Eastern
yarmulke
on his head,
he holds
a book of stories
in his hands,
turns
the pages
as he always did:
carefully,
respectfully,
leaning, learning
words the brain loses
before he under-
stands.

Esther Altshul Helfgott
Seattle, Washington

Aleppo's Gravedigger Died Yesterday

It doesn't matter
    who fired the rocket, only
        that he died fetching lamp oil

so he could see to dig
    by night as well as by day.
        He was buried in a grave he dug

that morning, not because it was needed,
    but as a preemptive strike
        against the daily surge of bodies.

He understood supply and demand,
    the economics of death that demanded
        he stockpile graves in neat rows,

one size fits all.
    Only last week his rough
        hands swung dust into neat piles

to the right of the graves. Now his son
    digs graves, the same neat piles to the right.
        Perhaps he digs his own grave.

Perhaps not, *inshallah*.

Vonnie Thompson
Monroe, Washington

Alexandria

if rupert murdoch believes something
if wall street wants to roll 1-sided dice
congress and/or parliament will sing harmony

if science and history are on sale what about all other
nonexperiential truths:
just cause it's on tv, on the web, in a newspaper—how did it get there?

do everything you can to save the libraries full of books.
you can't change books, you have to burn them

dan raphael
Portland, Oregon

Mumbai

We are standing parallel
to a hotel where the curtains are drawn.
It's early evening and the sun's fading away—
trace the stains in the sky with your fingertips.
We mirror a pair in the window, the one with curtains open.
The light behind them is too dark for you to see anything but their silhouettes:
"them," a man, a woman, but this is no embrace off the cover of a romance.
If anything, when she enfolds him in her hug and he starts shaking,
sobbing maybe on her shoulder, it feels like looking at Michelangelo's *Pieta*.

He starts crying a little,
and as if the man and woman in the window were merely projections
of our own future, I enfold him in a hug.
He's so thin. "Careful you don't break him," I hear a friend mocking
but that voice, low and faraway to me, comes only in retrospect,
because in this moment I don't think about thin, or small,
but vulnerable. Vulnerability, standing there in my arms
as I pat him on the back, whisper brief unmemorable consolations.
When I wake up I am happier than I have ever been
in dreams, or afterwards, within.

Adora Svitak
Redmond, Washington

Everywhere

Hungry Ghosts in America

have white hair
and Andy Warhol faces.
They run down the rain-splattered
post-midnight streets
wearing white sneakers,
baggy blue jeans,
oversized hooded sweatshirts,
calling out, "Quarter bags, quarter bags."
They used to be nickel bags and dime bags.
Inflation.
Inflation.
Overhead,
the low rumble of a jetliner
flying above the rain,
a silvery metallic body
above the silvery clouds
beneath the silvery moonlight.
Passenger 4D dines on chicken tetrazzini,
kahluha with
                milk and honey
                        roasted peanuts,
as he flies through the airspace of the Promised Land.

Kevin Mooneyham
Eugene, Oregon

Time Travel

We're in that not too distant future
that Andy Warhol predicted
where everyone is famous
for fifteen minutes or episodes

My plasma HD has grown
to dominate the wall
and my cell phone is
more television than telephone

The TV programming
is supposed to be
real people in real life
but it seems forced and contrived

It is like Warhol's work
derivative and repetitive
glamour airbrushed on
or car wreck . . . car wreck . . . car wreck

Terry Busch
Bothell, Washington

A Visit Home

Some say she was hit by a car
but I know different. She pulled over
by the side of the road
where she remembered
the pasture to be. She got out
to see if she could still hear
their laughter rolling around
in the grass. She and her sisters
playing horse, reins made of jump ropes
wrapped around each other's waists--
snorting, kicking, manes flying
running in circles
until their sides hurt
and they collapsed.
Then someone was honking,
yelling for her to move away
from the intersection.
That's when it happened,
the strip mall hit,
her heart stopped.

Erin Fristad
Port Townsend, Washington

Traveling Home

After eating, the men depart.
Tribal unity compels me to stay
in the warmth of the kitchen with
the women, cleaning as they talk with their icy tongues.

I am inept, knowing nothing of pie crusts,
crock pots, or meat loaf.
I am drawn in by the ritual, but sit apart
perched on a stool slowly sipping delicate wine.

The conversation turns to recipes and
I long to find the men, but my journey led me here, so I stay.
They take me on as their sport, a project.

I am trapped by ropes of recipes for
mashed-potato meat loaf and quick and easy pot roast.
I want to scream, "Enough.
This is a world I don't care to understand."

But I smile and reaching across the miles that separate us,
I accept recipes written neatly on note cards.
Later, on the backs of them, I will write poems.

Linda Thompson
Kenmore, Washington

The Cosmic Scholar

Secretary to the thoughts of others,
I grow, each night, to be the tenured scholar
of all galaxies. I gaze out
at the ancient history of stars—lights,
years old and centuries apart.
Anywhere we are, my text tells me,
is the center of a universe
on the exhale. Stars hurtle out
from every other star, like trees felled
by a meteor. They speed up
as they go—locomotives on an incline
or small boys sneaking out of school to fish.
If we caught up, the novas we've chased
would be old suns, ulcered with spots. . . .
By now I'm lost: the Horsehead Nebula's nostrils
quiver, I race Ferraris around Saturn's rings.
Before sleep, I shift down-spectrum—
blue to gold to red—and gather, soberly,
my scattered notes. Assembling once again
a face, like a chart of the periodic
elements, I leave it for the morning,
—the ditto sheets and cold white stares—
and follow the receding pulsars of the heart,
the stellar vapors reeling as I go. . . .

Carolyne Wright
Seattle, Washington

Here, we do second hand smoking well
It is my sole meditation technique
As I explore the internal architecture
Of a wrecked building
Or draw a cup of coffee
About to be consumed by a good citizen
Watching a slow apocalypse
I'm not sure about my rhythm yet
I know I'm somehow constrained
So I pretend to be sad
About the passing of time
And settle for these confessional poems
In hope they mirror someone's desire
To circumvent death

Maged Zaher
Seattle, Washington

The Plot God

The Plot God who lives in my shirt pocket
divulges nothing upon my command.
All day he crouches unseen, clutching
his collection of brilliant beginnings and ends,
even middles, reluctant to share.

Instead, he snickers,
beckons my story into box canyons,
pushes it off precipices.

I haul it out,
hang it up to dry,
and contemplate offerings:
My first-born protagonist;
My strongest action scene;
a magnificent mound of metaphors.

My pocket vibrates
with snores of
the Plot God.

Mary K. Whittington
Kirkland, Washington

Not Saying the F-Word

You can't say the F-word at Thin Man Books,
It's a amily-riendly bookstore, illed to the brim
with delicate ears. It's like a church, consecrated
to the Word that can't be spoken. Children, exotic
bonsai, are ertilized, pruned, and worshipped.

If you an't say the F-word then I'm almost
ertain you an't say the C-word either, but
you an probably say "suck" since every baby
does it and teenagers use it onstantly.
The vernacular for bowel movement is dicey.
Let's assume you an't ay the S-word
either. Makes it hard to tell "uck" like a baby
from "uck" the bad word, but better afe than orry.

That till leaves hundreds of thousands of words
with which to express yourself, so as my ather
used to ay, "quit your itchin'." Not exactly,
ut I uppose we an't ay the B-word either.
It's a amily-riendly ookstore, dedicated to
reedom of peech, and as poets our duty is to
e ourteous and not ay anything ontroversial.

Michael Schein
Carnation, Washington

American Sentences

10.10.02
Almost drowning out traffic noise, starlings in the Monkey Puzzle tree.

4.09.03
Maintenance man leaves a note says: . . . Can't fix your faucet its threads are striped.

9.24.04
Headline says: Body of Missing Sara Lee Executive Found Frozen.

6.15.05
At the ferry terminal her grocery list said: milk bread eggs stars.

5.20.06
Carolyne says: I don't know what to say and then she keeps on talking.

9.3.08
What I thought was Sam's zen golf concentration was his hearing aid turned off.

1.05.09
Would her Thanksgiving stuffing been this hard to flush had we eaten it?

3.29.10
Are female suicide bombers greeted in heaven by virgins too?

7.8.11
Stellar Jay—what? what? what? what? what? what? what? what? what? what? what? what? what?

1.15.13
Eighteen human heads found at O'Hare Airport have nothing to declare.

Paul E. Nelson
Seattle, Washington

Ephemeroptera

In that time, just a few remained
who asked why each bud of the rockrose
bloomed for just one day,
or why the female mayfly
winged up from lake-bound larval mud
only to die before she'd breathed the sky five minutes—
though not before mating and laying her silver-sac'd eggs
in the waters from which she'd just emerged—
or why the human eye so honors flames
and sunsets, those brief sculptures of orange
and crimson too soon subsumed
by ash or dusk. Or why the art
of grave digging had undergone a renaissance,
the earth perfumed with bodies adolescent, unbloomed.

Marjorie Manwaring
Seattle, Washington

Light

Once I caught light
and kept it in a box
beneath my bed.

Before long it wanted out,
so I taped the box shut.

Light was my secret.

But it made such
a great roar
that the darkness
shook.

Katherine Grace Bond
Mill Creek, Washington

Music Boxes from Aunt Jean

The great thing
about having five music boxes,
you can wind them all up
and sponsor competitions.
If families were music boxes
there'd be dogs leaping and
half-naked children, red-faced,
running around the house,
instead of plaster teddy bears
and spinning ballerinas.
Instead of earrings and bracelets
arranged on felt,
there'd be leftovers from
Thanksgiving dinners.
The music would be replaced
by bickering
that turns to laughter in an instant
and old anecdotes repeated
and laughed over
again.
If families were music boxes
each box would pick up
some of the music box melodies
it knew when it was young,
and then you'd take a few turns
of the mind
to remember
enduring, repeating fragments
of affection.

Richard Gold
Seattle, Washington

My New Truck

I was haulin' all my garbage to ah'r local dumpin' spot.
Seven cans o' garbage in the back o' my old Dodge.
Somethin' wasn't settin' right and really nagg'd on me,
So I went inside and cracked a beer in front o' my teevee.

This guy inside the teevee tube was talkin' 'bout his store.
Said they sell a hunnerd cars a day or mebbe even more.
Invited me to come on down—said all his cars was clean.
Swore he'd make me such a deal as one I never seen.

First thing they done showed me had a yeller racin' stripe.
They sicc'd me on a bright blue one but it jes' wasn't right.
Out there on the street was my fav'rite on the lot.
A candy-apple red 'un I just loved right on the spot.

I opened up my checkbook, threw in ever'thing I own.
I cain't believe they trust me with that 35-year loan.
The sticker shock I swaller'd wasn't half as hard to hold
As the shot my honey gimme when I drove that baby home.

My new custom-tailored pickup has a V-8 404,
An eight-disk CD changer and woofers in the doors,
A power-star transmission, chrome mags on every wheel.
Only thirty thousand bucks—I got me quite a deal.

She's quite a sight alright—them headlights sure are sweet,
Runnin' boards and mudflaps, carpet floors and velvet seats.
I keep her shined and spotless, an' she stays in my garage,
'Cause I still haul all my garbage t' the dump in my ol' Dodge.

Michael Heavener
Redmond, Washington

Peaches

Did you know that peaches speak?
    They do, but not too nicely,
teasing as I pass my fruit bowl
    morning, noon and nightly.
With a voice that's sugar sweet,
    attempting to entice me,
one whispers, "Come and hold me close.
    Your feverish touch excites me.
Why don't you have a little taste?
    You know how that delights me.
Just slide your tongue across my fuzz,
    and lick me, oh so lightly,
then kiss me with your burning lips,
    and bite me, bite me, bite me!"

Bill Hayes
Bellevue, Washington

Letting Go

I couldn't help but notice, my friend was slowing down,
and sometimes he would stumble as he slowly walked around.
The doctor ran a bunch of tests to find out what was wrong.
Cancer was the culprit, so he wouldn't live for long.

But with major surgery and chemotherapy too,
we might get him through the winter, what would you have us do?
Well, you've told me it's incurable and I see my friend's in pain,
to let him go on suffering to me seems inhumane.

What would life be without him, yet I knew I must decide.
With a heavy heart I made my choice as warm tears filled my eyes.
With my loving arms around him, I said "goodbye" for good,
then asked the doc to end his life, as gently as he could.

As the needle slid in, he slowly closed his eyes,
and his aches and pains all disappeared as in my arms he died.
So my faithful dog was put to sleep, humanely as could be.
I only ask, when it's my turn, please . . . do the same for me.

John Tripp
Redmond, Washington

Only You

Only you can know what aching silence
fills the rooms his voice so often shook;
only you can know what cold emptiness
sits in his chair, rests his side of the bed;
or when the curtain strokes your cheek
how clothes still lingering in the laundry pile
awake a fragrance seeping from the house,
leaving frozen spaces
where once he warmed your day.
Only you can know
when you turn the pages of his books,
hold his old sweater to your face,
take his toothbrush from the bathroom shelf,
how much you feel,
how much you cannot yet.

Ken Osborne
Redmond, Washington

Tori's Little Fascist Panties

"Those demigods with their nine-inch nails and little fascist panties tucked inside the heart of every nice girl"
—Tori Amos, "Precious Things"

Not those sleek cotton exercise panties that smooth over your mounds, the kind that say "these loins are girded."

Not those chaste white panties, a froth of satin and lace, meant to be worn as a token, a sacrifice.

Not those gag-store g-strings, just a swatch of cheap nylon and endless inches of scratchy elastic that rides up every crack and leaves welts where only a lover's kiss should be.

Nor Heather's high-priestess panties, practical, smooth and black, nary a ruffle nor a bow, instead a soft stripe of thong, cut not to titillate, but to frame.

No! Tori's fascist little panties are the ones fearful mothers buy for their daughters, hoping a drawer full of these will keep lusty thoughts at bay by keeping budding curves hidden behind a swaddle of tiny blue nosegays tied with impossibly cheerful bows. The kind that instantly fade to grey, then sag and droop, that even pedophiles would be hard-pressed to find attractive. The kind that develop tiny holes along the seams, the prim elastic edge fraying, looping around the button-fly in the wash, stretching and distending the cotton even more. The panties you're afraid you'll die wearing, knowing only the touch of bunchy cotton, damp with sweat and longing.

Dawn-Marie Oliver
Duvall, Washington

Make Him

The bruises inside my head are dark, purple, throbbing.

The words are blows, one after another. My voice is too loud, too harsh, I am too argumentative.

He cannot talk to me.

I don't listen, he says. He says it all.

When he is away, the children and I break eggs in the sink, use egg-beaters to make them foamy; add food coloring to see what happens. They wear little aprons I made as they stand on their chair at the sink. We make play clay and use cookie cutters; gather leaves and iron them between sheets of waxed paper.

When it is almost time for him to come home, the children get quieter. We clean up the mess, get ready for bed.

I can protect them. If he looks angry, I push the children behind me and back up toward the stairs.

I have nowhere to take them.

If you leave me you'll be sorry, he says.

I'm sorry I can't leave you, I think.

If you'd just do things my way, the right way, it would be fine, he says.

But it's never fine. The bruises in my head grow larger.

One day my son looks at me and says, "I wish you would make him go away."

I will try, my baby.

Heather Stark
Woodinville, Washington

Recovery Girl

(for Daria)

Recovery girl
takes her first few steps
on the tight-rope stretched over
relapse canyon.
Loved ones
hold their breath for her
needing to help
knowing they must not.

There's little confidence
inside Recovery Girl
She must trust words
from an invisible coach,
ignore how naked
how alone she feels.
And she must fight
with every thread in her soul
the irresistible urge
to look down.

Christopher J. Jarmick
Kenmore, Washington

The Healing Restaurant

For Joy, a dear friend and a great teacher.

In my dream you attach a news clipping to my papers
On the visor of the passenger side of my Honda
About an old man from my family
Who I was thinking to privately forgive.

The newsprint heralds the undoing of my writing
My chronicle of days, my log of woes
Pages disturbed, turned every which way
My wounds are revealed for all to see

And I haven't even read the clipping.

In my dream you take me out to eat
Only one menu comes, and you give it to me
There are two options:
Be Done Good By or Take Care and Let Go.

Holding tight to my disturbed pages, I order Number 1
Perhaps I am not ready to forgive after all.
The waiter brings me a steaming bowl of miso soup
I devour it.

In my dream the old man from the news
His back against the wall, no soup or surface to speak of,
Gazes outward from dead eyes, watches us,
Too many patrons to count.

I am by no means alone.

Pamela Denchfield
Duvall, Washington

Emergency Comfort Kit

Inside, we should place a blanket, one that folds to the size
of a toy kazoo. A light stick, the kind kids love

to swirl at the darkening sky. He needed six hand wipes,
a pack of Kleenex, his name on a 3 x 5 card.

A small cozy toy made sense; we knew which ones
we couldn't take away, but the one he would need that day—

which? The thirty-gallon trash bag: a poncho of course.
A family photo—*for comfort*—but also identification.

We were to tell ourselves these were ordinary measures,
thoughts to store away in the bottom-most drawer,

on the farthest, most unreachable shelf. That the likelihood
of needing the raisins was slim, that even when a blizzard

disabled all our county's buses, most of the children
slept that night in their beds. This was routine,

and the cans of apple juice would never be punctured,
and the letter, like the looks on our faces,

would never be read.

Martha Silano
Seattle, Washington

who invented this moonlit land filled with
work which changes nature, but not life &
never the nature of man? this immutable nature
of man as work & the anthropology of work or dream.
body art quicksilver medication, restless
nights filled with roosting crows, frustrated
by reality he turns to his dreams.
This whole land is void of laughter. the
drear fog of winter settled in from the people's
eyes. she had had the last laugh back somewhere
in late August, perhaps early September, when
the salmon, when the blue backs look up the creek.
that was the last time they had laughed
& he couldn't remember why or how their world
had gone so serious. where had it gone? where
was the glint of the fish? the warmth of the
fire? the changing of the tide? get back to work.
that is our only advice—& the last laugh still
won't return. we begin to think that this
last laugh thing is pretty serious. we never
really expected to witness the last laugh—
to see it spent so frivolously, so lightly.
just who is it has the last laugh? we could
use it back (you know). kind of like a hair ball
or bad food, coyote's pretty sure
whoever has it should just cough it up.

David Lloyd Whited
Vashon, Washington

A Blessing (Sunflower)

May you continue to give graces
And bloom again next year
The bride will want to see you
Growing tall in the golden field
May your head be high
And small creatures
Lift you up with their sweetness
Though they may crawl through life
We are all born with wings

Monica Schley
Seattle, Washington

Dandelion

My daughter and I wrote a poem last night
We picked ideas and objects to write about
We mixed them up
in a salad bowl
carefully tossed

We picked funny words
to make happy sounds
We added, repeated, deleted
We laughed and fell to our toes
pretended to be dandelions
waiting for the wind
to shake us up

We acted like daffodils
and tulips soaked in rain
We opened ourselves in the morning
and closed our petals
when the sun ran away
We agreed that our poem
should be like a dandelion
so when shared with others
the words will float to the ears
of those who listen

Carried by our breath
like the dandelion fuzzes
in the breeze
and so my daughter and I
wrote a poem last night

Raúl Sánchez
Seattle, Washington

Discovering the Tasmanian Devil Is My Life Coach

He wants me to speak without language.
What can you say in a facial expression?
Can you find contentment in chaos? Disruption?

All my life I've been told
to speak slowly, use manners.
He'd like me to slurp a hunk of meat

from my dinner plate, break the wine glass
and guzzle the bottle. He says I'm improving
on my spontaneity, but there's room

to rip apart the wildflowers without feeling
guilty for what was. He says remember the time
your mother said young ladies don't dress that way.

He tells me to spin naked through a continent
being distracted only with rabbits disguised
as the opposite sex. Try dressing as a tornado,

find passion in every twirl.
He tells me he knows it's silly
to suggest I sleep on a full stomach

and destroy whatever gets in my path,
but he's asked me to be an innocent savage,
be the person the room stops for.

Kelli Russell Agodon
Kingston, Washington

Advice Left Between the Pages of Grimms'

Life is not a fairy tale, and this isn't your pumpkin coach.
You're not lost in some magic wood,
and that blood on your hands isn't from an innocent stag
at all. Princess, remember to fill your pockets
with more than bread crumbs, and
if you can't sleep, don't blame the legumes
beneath the sheets. One look at that glass coffin
they've set up should tell you everything
you need to know about their intentions.
Remember a lot of girls end up dismembered, and
every briar rose has its thorn.
Forget the sword and magic stone,
forget enchantments and focus on the profit margin,
the hard line. Read the subtext.

Jeannine Hall Gailey
Redmond, Washington

Let It Be

Raw, lucid
no diaphanous sheen, just
pure snow, just sun brightness
focused through crystal, words
tumbling like Milky Way stars
in the curvature of earth or
an ampersand of wave,
let it be blood, let it be wine,
let it be fire hot enough to
bend steel, crack stone,
or if air the kind that sets birds free,
a snowy owl perhaps, eyes
keen, wings splayed out in full.

William Scott Galasso
Edmonds, Washington

Trapped

When the elevator stops between floors,
the woman in the grey suit,
with pinching red heels
and hair lacquered shut,
dreams the same dream
as the dough-faced messenger boy,
sweat already beading his upper lip, manila envelope
turning to oatmeal in his nervous fingers.

Together they fly about the tiny cage,
a mismatched pair of parakeets
awaiting the sweet old lady in the tea-stained apron
to pull off the cloth and call forth the day,
the way a magician pulls one rabbit after another
out of the same impossibly small hat,
or rejoins the severed halves of a woman
making her again whole.

Lana Hechtman Ayers
Kingston, Washington

The Chickadee

A lone chickadee
on a dead pine trunk
disapprovingly
eyes the woods—
spring spy?

Next morning
the world tweeted
"Snow in spring
Snow in spring."

But he,
he just knew it
sitting there
analyzing
spring air.

He came back
shook his head
looked stern
finished his
weather report,
fluttered away.

Aarthi John
Redmond, Washington

Songbird

On Shabbat, the heft of my mother's baritone shatters
the windows, whistles the reds of (almost) sunset to our table
silvered with wine cup, candlesticks, tray of challah.
We light the candles, float our hands over flame, cover
our eyes, my sister and I peeking, giggling, waiting
for my mother to quake the chandelier and crash it
like an elk head into the kugel—ooze of noodles, nutmeg,
raisins; crust, a little too burnt (when will she learn?).
It's happened before.
My mother wears her song like a bow tie, sometimes plaid
sometimes crooked. She could be a cantor, lead a choir,
opera star—roles like Carmen, Butterfly, Aida.
Instead, she powers it in the shower, in shul, at home on Shabbat,
reruns of South Pacific—"I'm Gonna Wash that Man
Right Out of My Hair." Scrubs her scalp, a smile that wilds
her quietude, inspires me to belt it out with her, shatter
the windows, too. Dance in bare feet on the buttercup rug
and cheer as the chandelier crashes.

Ann Teplick
Seattle, Washington

Going—

I photograph you every morning
In a cruel attempt to capture
A formal souvenir of what I love
After breakfast, and then
Each day a little less
You take a stand, examine finches
Windowpanes   knocking
Your head against my hand
Until you don't—
There is no way to tell you
That you are going
With few days left
For what our rebel hearts relay

Susan Rich
Seattle, Washington

Snoozer

Black cat on purple pillow nestles, curls
Above each golden-tassled corner. Snooze,
Oh king of slink, oh prince of pounce, oh whirl
Of fur, oblivious to gossip, news,
And faction. Dukes and countesses and earls
Might battle; you chase mouse and string, refuse
To yield, except as weariness might win.
And even then: you sleep but seem to grin.

David D. Horowitz
Seattle, Washington

The Raccoon

I came to your house for sympathy, but there were test tubes in the way, distilled water, and all kinds of machines staring me in the face.

I went to your studio and only a raccoon sat in the corner next to the rocking chair, looking unoccupied and uncomfortable.

I left and went for a walk, but it was too cold.

I went to jump in the ocean, but it was too hot.

I walked under the bridge to gather stones to put on my grave, but they slipped out of my fingers on the way up the hill.

I stopped to watch the sun set behind the mountains, but it rose instead and floated sideways over my head.

I went back to your house and the test tubes were smashed, steam oozing out of the broken pieces and floating out the windows.

I went back to your studio and the raccoon was watching you sitting in another corner, eating a bowl of salt water with a fork.

I went to dip my finger in the bowl, but it was too hot.

I wanted to stay in the room, but it was too cold.

Finally, you spoke to me, stones of wisdom to put on my grave.

I cried, and my tears filled the empty bowl with warm salt water.

The sun burst through the door, and the raccoon smiled in the corner.

Leslie Brown
Redmond, Washington

Summer Day

Trailing blackberries entwined
with juicy, ripe salal
set off the robins
into a hip-hop dance.

Cotton tails yawn,
munch, yawn,
blinking at
the alfalfa butterfly
repeatedly kissing
a glass door.

An undaunted mule deer
takes a stroll—
her fawn follows in
veneration.

Sunlight sears into the thicket.
Pink starflowers
silently in love,
shine.

Aarthi John
Redmond, Washington

The Old Mare

May

On a warm Sunday morning,
I walk by the silver-haired horse
and stop to share the day.
She munches the grass
with a low grinding sound
taking a half step forward now and then
here and there.
No longer frisky
she is further calmed
by the tranquilizer pellets that her owner,
now not so young herself anymore
and a little dotty,
feeds her to deal with her moody needs.
I look into her wet dark eyes
and see my future.

October

It's a blustery Sunday morning.
The silver haired mare has disappeared.
The swaying brown grass in the field is knee high
with no horse to pull and chomp.
Her old owner,
bending over, still in her tan riding pants,
weeds the front lawn alone.
They were friends for thirty years.
The blue tarp covering something over there flaps;
flaps in the wind.
Looks like they're going to sell the house.

Peggy Barnett
Woodinville, Washington

The Wolf's Appetite

As I began to eat
Your grandmother—
Starting with her coarse pink feet,
Her face collapsing like a pale puckering currant,
Her eyes a fierce Cerulean blue—
She regarded me sadly, as if her fate were unavoidable.

She opened her mouth
But no cries came, only the soft piping of a flute.

Yet when I had eaten up to her waist
Her bony arms leapt through her nightshirt
And she gouged my eyes with her eagle claws,
No longer hands with old-crone knuckles and nails
But talons, with a life of their own.

I should have eaten her hands first.

Laura Lee Bennett
Redmond, Washington

Mrs. Coyote must be authentic at all times; at least
all her furs are real. ratty old mothballed
coyote itchy skin. coyote ugly. always just woke up.

in church coyote hears the word, not to be confused
with truth or something that will surely happen.
at the big white downtown church Coyote slinks
into his pew (sort of a supernatural walk)
& when they pass the plate, when that collection plate
comes by, he sticks in his paw and pulls out a bill
or two, out comes a draw, he considers it a gift
a kind of potlatch loan for his endurance of the word.
When he sees all that money his tail fluffs up, all
those green frog skins make his eyes remember the birds
& his eyes glitter silver & green gold. his palms sweat.
amid all those good intentions & Christian charity.
Mrs. Coyote is a long-suffering soul & patient beyond
any reckoning. Yes, she's heard all of the stories
but has never been able to bring herself to believe.
She's probably in deep denial, but she cries a lot at night
& hopes that her pups will never hear those awful rumors.
She harbors great compassion & prefers not to discuss
her husband's convictions. at least not his latest one.

David Lloyd Whited
Vashon, Washington

Increment Weather

the light changes so gradually the clock needs only 3 or 4 numbers—
increment weather—mist,   drizzle,   showers,   rain
no matter how thin, how quick, how protected by internal heat
you get the rain's message, a spamming no firewall or antivirus can stop,
no silver bullet can protect your thirst, maintain the crispness of cuffs or pastry

speed doesn't affect saturation; waterproof only means the rain will come from in you
everyone votes, everyone drinks, everyone feels what could be tears   drool
              leakage that has no name but you still feel responsible for
we're born wet & die wet, releasing what we've hoarded

if we could see the stars they'd be milky smears on the inside of our galactic umbrella

why have a roof?   why taunt thirst with windows?
is plumbing a false god?   do toilets mean we're ashamed of our inefficiency?
to pay for water means you're not free, to drink imported water from a plastic bottle
means you're no longer completely human, compromised by living so long
with so many thirsty strangers

dan raphael
Portland, Oregon

Pop-Rocks in Church

Make a joyful noise unto your lord.
So why not pop-rocks?
Why not celebrate a deity with
Playful, happy noises,
Tasting not of bitter wine and
Dime-store paste?
Rather with sweet grape and strawberry sparks?

I want a god who
Delights in pleasure,
Urges us to enjoy.
Not one who demands
Denial in somber tones.

Come, eat your pop-rocks
Washed down with cherry cola.
Make a truly
Joyful noise unto
Your own lord.

Dawn-Marie Oliver
Duvall, Washington

Merry-Go-Round

Sunday at two
on the merry-go-round.
My father's camera preserved the scene
in black and white,
but now, with
his photograph in my hand,

I am six again,
astride my golden steed,
my fingers gripping
the gleaming pole,
spiraling upward
through the roof,
my mount surging forward,
and dropping back, while
the carousel organ blares.

We're racing the black horse behind,
the bay to our left,
as the green of the park flows past
in a ribbon of color, blurring
my father, my mother,
my grandmother waving her gloves.

I wish I could gallop upon my steed
forever. And in a way,
we're galloping still
in this photograph
here in my hand.

Mary K. Whittington
Kirkland, Washington

Still Day

Sittin' here thinkin' on the day.
Pretty quiet.
A lot like last week
and tomorrow
and yesterday.

Sittin' here itchin' for what to do and why.
No have to's.
None seem to be comin'
seen none passin' by.

Havin' trouble finding my way
Can't seem to rustle up a story
on this grey sky shiny day.

Talked to someone yesterday.
Believe it was a woman.

Didn't have much to say.

Wendelle Peoples
Everett, Washington

This Morning

"Light takes the Tree; but who can tell us how?"
—*Theodore Roethke*

It's time. It's almost too late.
Did you see the magnolia light its pink fires?
You could be your own, unknown self.
No one is keeping it from you.

The magnolia lights its pink fires,
daffodils shed papery sheaths.
No one is keeping you from it—
your church of window, pen, and morning.

Daffodils undress, shed papery sheaths—
gestures invisible to the eye.
In the church of window, pen, and morning
what unfolds at frequencies we can't see?

Gestures invisible to naked eye,
the garden opens, an untranslatable book
written at a frequency we can't see.
Not a psalm, exactly, but a segue.

The garden opens, an untranslatable book.
You can be your own, unknown self—
not a psalm, but a segue.
It's time.

Elizabeth Austen
Seattle, Washington

Friday Night

With a flash of white
an eagle splits
the seamless gray
of sky
and river in the rain.

At your house
the key sits on a dusty beam,
the kettle steeps with tea.
Coals in the stove stoked
with white grain alder
uprooted in another winter,
dried to perfection
in a blazing summer sun.
Quiet taps of heat expanding glowing flames
against dark red walls
burn deeply into blackness of the night.
Clothes peeled,
Two more blankets piled on my side
burrowed down with steaming mug and book
into soft gold light.

I dissolve into the echo of the rain upon the roof.

By what unlikely stroke of grace
does this define a life?

Mary Eliza Crane
Duvall, Washington

Philosophy Test

I forget her name now, though I think it started with a C. We both sat in the back row, she in the left corner, me in the middle. I forget the teacher's name, too, but remember that the subject was Western philosophy.

> a robin's song . . .
> she turns in her midterm
> just before me

The news ripples through the dorms after the weekend. Heading home on Friday night, near Pasco, she crossed the center line. She was by herself. They said it was instant.

> dorm fireplace—
> someone asks
> if God really exists

At class again on Monday, the teacher repeats the news. A few gasps. For those not on campus, it's the first they've heard. The professor hands back all our midterms, tells us that she got a C. "Sorry if this is hard to read," he says she wrote, "but my pen was running out of ink."

> I turn to the last page
> to see my test score—
> the corner seat, empty

Michael Dylan Welch
Sammamish, Washington

InDependence

I want to ask her
Standing there by stovetop
Over Sunday's pumpkin pancakes,
Her cotton pajamas
Pearly white with red petals,

I want to ask her
About the dogged curiosity
That marbles her personality.

I want to ask her
How she ventured
Into painting clouds
On the walls
Of the downstairs bathroom,
Delicate transparent puffs
Of cumulus wafting
Below the ceiling.

I want to ask her
To love me forever,
To dance a two-step,
A foxtrot, a tango,
Through dances of
Fear and doubt,
To rescue me
From these
Indecipherable mutters.

Tom Flynn
Redmond, Washington

The Last Two Weeks

I haven't heard him speak
a word
in the last two weeks
but today
when we were sitting
together
in the quiet
of an out-of-the-way
room
after I finished
cutting his mustache
and beard
he said:
I'm sorry, honey.
As if he knew exactly
what we'd gone through
all these years.

Esther Altshul Helfgott
Seattle, Washington

Seen and Unseen

my feet tapping the floor
of gravity's heartbeat

a wasp nest hung to decorate the rafters
by the salad tongs of diversity

the path of sunlight across the table, up the wall, and disappearing
into the emotional upheaval of dandelions

bamboo leaves swaying, green against yellow stalks,
against the tension of sky

the smell of coffee breath puffed from your mouth
like memory's garden hose

unlit Christmas lights along the eave
through the conjugation of fritillaries

mistaking a birdbath for a sundial at noon
while capillaries disagree on the nature of God

stones crunching under my Birkenstocks
beside the antlers of memory

flagstones cracked by tiny flowers,
by abstract definitions of hate

a rope swing silent though I expect a creak
while the muse blows its nose

the black sound of the crow beyond the copse
a home for wonder

Michael Dylan Welch
Sammamish, Washington

Epiphanette

Babies are just like people, without the opinions.
At fifteen months, my daughter presses her palms
to either side of her face, pushing inward and forward,
shuddering with exertion before she announces,
"I cannot take my face off. It's stuck,"
and I get to watch
as her carefree cognitive tumbleweed
is struck by the SUV of enlightenment,
being still baby-receptive to the fairy-godmother-
magic-wand boink of epiphany. *La-la-la,*
sings her puff-ball brain
as it bobs on the breeze of her senses,
or that's how it looks from the patch of ground
I've dug myself into, stuck to my root ball of views
about social media, conceptual art, and the use of *comprise.*
Now she braces the heels of her hands
under each side of her jaw and pushes straight up.
Her conclusion: "My head is stuck too."
Already she baby-knows:
A dance you learn; the dancer you're stuck to.
Meanwhile, my mother comes more and more unstuck
from the sticky-note balaclava of knowledge and memory
that once made her brain a grown-up brain.
One by one, the engrams detach and zip
off into infinity, spastically flapping like butterflies
caught in senility's hurricane headwind—
a parody of a dance—while my daughter,
all dancer, takes her first position.

Dennis Caswell
Woodinvilllle, Washington

Jessie

Here comes Jessie down the hall,
bumping up against the wall
    and dragging Teddy by one foot.
    I wonder where that child has put
her missing sock . . . her other shoe?
I'm sure she started out with two.
    She slips and slides across the floor
    then pauses, with a smile before
she reaches for my slice of bread,
as I say "No," and shake my head.
    With three sweet kisses for a trade,
    Jessie soon has marmalade
from cheek to cheek and down her chin.
She charms me with a sticky grin,
    spins around then pats her tummy,
    hugs me close and tells me, "Yummy."
As she squirms, and laughs with glee
I kiss one freckled, dimpled knee,
    then ease the tangles from her hair.
    She loves her big-girl underwear
which is a challenge, I agree,
as Jessie isn't quite yet three.
    But after splashing in the tub,
    with giggling games of "rub-a-dub,"
her wondrous smile completely charms,
as I take her in my arms,
    and as she nods, then falls asleep . . .
    my love for Jessie makes me weep.

Bill Hayes
Bellevue, Washington

Breath

You were so tiny.
                    I watched you sleep

just to see the rise and fall
                    of your breath, afraid

if I looked away it would stop.
                    I cradled you in my arms

let you sleep, that breath
                    a safe rhythm on my neck.

Now not even your hat fits me,
                    sliding low over eyes that still watch

for the rise and fall of covers.
                    I breathe breath to breath with you.

You don't wake. I am still
                    afraid to look away.

Vonnie Thompson
Monroe, Washington

when someone says i love you and means it

their hair beard and fingernails grow faster
their sense of humor and universe expands
policemen smile at them their subatomic
vibration flows at a higher frequency result-
ing in weight loss more laughter heightened
intuition and appetite suppressant a career in
the military is less likely poetic inhibitions
are reduced short flights of fancy likely the
weather improves small irritations disappear
shades of pink and green glow around them
their shoes stop squeaking trees begin to talk
to them invitations to dinner parties multiply
exponentially cats purr around them bowel
movements become effortless their dreams
more vivid less disturbing sleep comes easily
less is needed news does not distract know-
ledge loses power the future less important
investments appear ludicrous lips swell eyes
dilate throat chakras open creative powers
return play defeats work circulation improves
their life force is strong and undemanding

Stephen Roxborough
Anacortes, Washington

Success Bomb #45

"She stared at ruin. Ruin stared straight back."

Divested of her armor of thrift-store duds
Eulene's the success bomb, striking minor
triumphs, like enemies, off her hit list.
Lounging in the bathtub's bubbly suds
for hours, she plays "Start Me Up" on her
CD player a hundred times till her best

bodacious parts are wrinkly as gin-
stewed prunes. "What, we hurry?" Eulene
growls, between the subwoofer's thudding booms
and the rhetorical popping of bonbons
into her lip-glossed kisser. "Ah!" she moans,
and palms, like an oracle, the H_2O stains

blessing her e-book of Berryman's Dream Songs—whichever
18 lines of frantic jabber her finger
lands on: her next career move! Then: horrors!
The e-book slips from her grasp, disappears
sub-bubblewards. Electrifying revelation!
Eulene's last flash as the jobless dark comes un-

Carolyne Wright
Seattle, Washington

Menarche

Amy got her period just now.
Shut the door; don't let the others hear.
The boys will never let her live it down.

Miss Shepherd says she is a woman now.
She says it hurts. The stains won't disappear.
Amy got her period just now.

Don't let them hear you; howl without a sound,
your strength, your power safely wrapped in fear
the boys will never let you live it down.

I'm scared that when mine comes I won't know how.
She's older than I am by just one year
and Amy got her period just now.

We'll all stay close, a wall of girls around
so nobody can smell the blood and tears.
The boys will never let her live it down.

This water's deep enough for us to drown.
with boys like gators, grinning ear to ear,
Amy got her period just now.
and they will never, ever, never, ever, never, never, never,
they will never let us live it down.

Rebecca Meredith
Seattle, Washington

Leaving

I feel the ping
of a neuron
firing and missing
leaving
the thought behind,

like I left my cell phone
sitting on my bedside table,
as the estrogen flows out
leaving
a thin soggy layer,

of menopause
washed across my chest
sticking to my shirt
leaving
chilled goose bumps,

over the sag of skin
like thin rice paper
damp and rippling
leaving
wrinkles in places,

I never expected

Elizabeth Carroll Hayden
Bellevue, Washington

Inversion

I press my palm against
Mother's forehead to
check for a fever.

Cora Goss-Grubbs
Woodinville, Washington

Mother's Day Rose Bush

Year after year, I tended it:
Fertilized, pruned. Deep-watered the roots.
Breathed the scent of blossoms, remembering
your love, your thoughtfulness,
your frailties.

Year after year, I trickled
soapy water over aphids, plucked off leaves—
black-spotted, insect-bitten—destroyed them.
Assailed by summer heat and winter frost,
the bush grew weaker. But
roses still bloomed.

Early this year, I touched brittle lichen-crusted
limbs. Weather and pests
had won the battle.
I hacked away dead wood, leaving two
stems, too thick for clippers.

April, May passed. Then in early June,
on the foot-high sticks, leaves sprouted.
Healthy, strong.

I touch the new buds, grateful for
another year of roses.
We can't choose our miracles.

Marie Helen Turner
Playa Vista, California

Mother's Smile

Mother smiles,
An expression her grandmother,
Dead twenty years before I was born,
Might recognize.

Perhaps she
Is who the smile is for.

I smile back,
Wondering who she sees.
It would be selfish
To wish it was me.

Janka Hobbs
Kirkland, Washington

Mama's Five Cents

Mama received five cents on her fifth birthday,
Given by a relative visiting from far away,
Filled with joy, she dashed to the village market right away.
Flashed in her mind was a conversation she had
with a villager who reads books all day.
"What's in a book?" Mama asked.
"Many things," smiled the villager.
"There's beauty.
There is treasure.
You can read for knowledge or pleasure.
If you wish, you may see the whole world with leisure."
"Is that SO?" Mama gasped.
She sensed the wonder and made a wish.
Zip, zip, zoom, zoom!
As she reached the bookstand in the market,
She put her money on the counter and said,
"A book please!"
The book keeper, an old man with heavy glasses,
Examined Mama through his thick lenses,
Without looking at the coin, he handed her a book,
"Here you are, my child, enjoy it as you wish!"

Qiaolan Wan
Redmond, Washington

Ritual

For a dying mother

Feather yourself on the edge of the bed, yellow
with rose-quilted pillows. Fold into her atrophy,
be the leaven, like egg white into batter. Kiss her
while she winces, cries, bedsores the size
of "Why me? Why me?"
Listen to her words. "How could I love you?"
Cup the silence. Let it float, hum. Be the puff
of dandelion seed. There are no answers.
Canoe her through lotus and fog; the lake, milky with silver.
Hallucinate with her: her mother trellising pie crust,
her father butchering cows.
Listen to her words. "Why should I love you?"
Watch the bile projectile from her lips,
there are no questions. Sponge her face,
the washcloth scrunched. Peel the nightgown
that mummies her, flocks of bunnies in pink pastel.
Unveil her 84-year-old body, chunks cut away,
grated and charred. Slip on a fresh one, doilies around the collar.
Listen to her words. "I couldn't have loved you."
Be still. Iron the thunder. Stop wondering
how long this dying will take. Be still. Separate *her* pain
from *yours*. Be still, the chicken wing stuck in your throat
will fly to Barbados, where she buried her shame.
Listen to her words. "I tried not to love you."
Lullaby her with the Beatles. Remember the day
she walked you to the record shop and bought your first 45,
"She Loves You." Yeah, yeah—*yeah*—but now,
there are no harmonies to sleep with. It's easy.
Love her, love her, love her.

Ann Teplick
Seattle, Washington

A Mother's Mantra

I'm sorry when the milk's run dry, sorry the bath's too hot, sorry for the drafty diaper changes, the fever, the insensitive doctor who ordered a catheter when you were just four months old. I'm sorry for being tired and impatient and interrupting your block play with dinner. Did you hear my apology for the open gate that didn't stop your fall? I think you understand now: the hurried goodbyes, the peanut butter sandwich cut the wrong way, the zipped neck skin and skinned knees. I've stopped saying it out loud: the playdate cut short, the arm tug out of harm's way, the no's to candy and ice cream and screen time and another round of knock knock who's there. I might as well say it now for the teasing, the lost tooth, lost friendship, loss of innocence, for your first kiss, it will not be what you expect. I'm sorry a thousand sorries for the first time your heart is broken. Trust me, it won't be the last.

Cora Goss-Grubbs
Woodinville, Washington

Myth

I buried my father
down by the river
chill winter morning
stilled by my grief.

He has become myth
like famine,
rebellion,
like great blue heron,
who came to me here
and stayed by my side
through the months of his dying,
blown down by the wind,
browned like a leaf
to this silence.

Mary Eliza Crane
Duvall, Washington

Requiem for My Father, May 2001

My father died
    inward
from the extremities.
Blood pooled
    in the basement
        layers
of his dormant legs
like water from
a broken main
in a vacant cellar.
The wiring in his
    weedy suburbs
    arced and shorted out.
His inner city,
    fortified by
    cardboard and
        peeling paint,
held to the last
its central power,
    stronger than it
        should have been,
a bluish light
that struggled
and gave up its heat
all at once
when it realized
no one
lived there
any longer.

Beth Atwood
Redmond, Washington

After the Funeral

On listening to the recording of my mother's funeral

Plastic words on a plastic tape,
so much unsaid and so much I never knew,
a stranger's voice telling your life's tale
circuiting with care the sad disgrace
making you seem a gentle person now
who I can hardly recognize from stilted words
my mind still locked in childhood rooms
of railing bitterness and hate
where like my father I had turned my back:
arrived too late this time to say goodbye.
Tears came more than I ever thought,
glimpsing again the gentle happier days
that I had lost and came too late to save.
Is this what death must bring to me, regret
spun with sadness from a plastic reel,
to learn at last how much I truly feel?

Ken Osborne
Redmond, Washington

Bill's Ashes

I'm glad his ashes weren't spread
at sea, and though he liked to sail,
he chose instead to have them thrown
to earth like seeds, along a trail
that cut through ferns and led

to a forgotten grotto where
novitiates once knelt in shade,
whose mingled murmurings were known
to linger, and the prayers they made,
still interrupt the evening air.

I'm glad he picked a spot on land
that we could reach by foot, come back
to visit time-to-time, take deep
breaths, have thoughts that fill the lack
of him we scattered here by hand.

The eight of us in ones and twos,
we dusted ferns, we powdered moss
between the trees and then to keep
his ghost alive and staunch our loss,
went home, his ashes on our shoes.

Donald Kentop
Seattle, Washington

Smoke

A tribute to Grandma Carmen

She swiftly brushed my body
with *ramas de pirú* and flowers
red ribbon held the willow branches
she brushed, brushed, brushed away
my stretched limbs
bad energy away from me
fragrant sap remained
on fingers dark from cutting

herbs frankincense chunks
burning *copal.*
Top, down, left, right
her eyes closed cleansing smoke
branches swirled
the smoke with every stroke
shaking filtering negative energy
the room full of smoke

cleansing smoke
chasing evil spells
silent prayer whisper
echoed through the smoke
she opened her eyes
two moons behind the clouds.
She wrapped the loaded branches
told me to throw it behind my back

and walk away
into the light.

Raúl Sánchez
Seattle, Washington

Finishing It

Smoke drifts down damp trunks of hemlock.
It rains all night. The thin soil thins a little more.
Nothing is rapid. Trees block and bend
the light. His pocket watch is losing days.

Good as dead, the doctors cannot save him.
The shaman cannot clear his throat.
Spurning hospice, he plays poker on the phone.
It's why he fishes—to feel the panic in his hands.

Bill Yake
Olympia, Washington

remember when we were all water?

perfect charged elastic pure
serene crystal rain
fluid and flowing as the magic stream
in all the ancient stories

we made our own light then
and reflected everything
floated over the timeless dream
splashed away and returned

we tumbled whirled and crashed
without fear or harm
effortlessly bent and reshaped
every landscape

unhurried yet gushing together
running as one
we could drink each other
and only get stronger

Stephen Roxborough
Anacortes, Washington

Praising the Fish

You are the visible whispering one.
The Brahmin. You are the flush of blood
behind a thin skin of mirrors. Your scales
are small as single notes. Rainbow above all

rainbows, you are jaw and composure.
At sunset your tail is broad. It propels
you up glistening into burning skies,
gills pulsing and nose to the wind as if

it were current. It is

the way wheat-land sunsets burn rivers.
In the flash behind flesh and the blush under
cutbanks, you are the rainbow of horizon,
thunderhead, creek braid and plunge pool.

You are frost turning the sun green.
And buoyed by an aspirated clarity—
all this air within water within air—
you are a towering splash of hunger,

our flourishing, transient shout.

Bill Yake
Olympia, Washington

The Hatch

The hatch is all around us,
a frothing boil of wings
rising out of the water.
Mayflies dodge the trout below,
drift in clouds down the river.

Perhaps this morning, this afternoon,
all the nymphs at the bottom stopped,
looked,
up to the sun
and swam to the surface,
all together,
up, up into the sky, unfolding dried wings just in time.

Then, the change.
Dancing and dipping,
a touch,
a kiss,
the long fall,
the only sound is us, wading through the shallows,
casting, casting.

Ana Christensen
Montlake Terrace, Washington

The World to Come

Let's say we make our own happiness, roll over
in the fields, stain our arms and legs with blue

grass; let's say there's simply one year left
to draw lists of clouds, slip guilt free through bars

of chocolate, hold each other in this black hole
of restlessness. This life.
Tonight we will battle the linoleum squares,
laundry stairs, glass deck where one day

the body is sure to grab its last hungry breath.
What if all that's left for us is gravity,

canned soup, a shimmer of thinning hair?
Let's say we make our own happiness even so—

the tail swoop of katsura trees, triple shots
of strong coffee, a folded map—

Then may I remember to thank the academy
of daily minutiae: suitcases, car keys, a friend's

first novel of karaoke. Who says we can't
have it all: the house of sky and soft catcalls—

Who says we can't find another way
to fail, to come up short, to catch and release.

Susan Rich
Seattle, Washington

Publication Credits

Poems not listed here are previously unpublished.

Kelli Russell Agodon: "Discovering the Tasmanian Devil Is My Life Coach" and "If I Ever Mistake You for a Poem," *Letters from the Emily Dickinson Room*, Buffalo, New York: White Pine Press, 2010.

Elizabeth Atwood: "Orkney Equinox" and "Requiem for My Father, May 2001 #2," *The Skeleton Concerto: Poems in Three Movements*, Redmond, Washington: Blackwing Press, 2005.

Elizabeth Austen: "Leaving the Island," *Sightlines*, Chappaqua, New York: Toadlily Press, 2010. "This Morning," *Pontoon #7*, Floating Bridge Press, 2004.

Lana Hechtman Ayers: "Dorothy Does Italy" and "Trapped," *Chicken Farmer I Still Love You*, Indian Trail, North Carolina: D-N Publishing, 2007.

Peggy Barnett: "The Old Mare" and "The Longest Word," *On Your Left*, Woodinville, Washington: Clara Bear Publishing, 2013. "The Longest Word" was written at RASP's island-style slam on December 3, 2010 using three words provided by Michael Dylan Welch ("antidiestablishmentarianism," "scrumptious," and "hydrogen"), thus earning the distinction of being this anthology's only poem written *at* a RASP event.

Janée J. Baugher: "Old Woman Dying," *The Body's Physics*, Huntington Beach, California: Tebot Bach, 2013.

Leslie Brown: "The Raccoon," in senior thesis, University of Santa Cruz, Santa Cruz, California: June 1977.

Dennis Caswell: "Epiphanette" and "This," *Phlogiston*, Seattle, Washington: Floating Bridge Press, 2012.

Mary Eliza Crane: "Myth," *Quill and Parchment*, June 2011 (online). "Friday Night," *At First Light*, Fayetteville, Arkansas: Gazoobi Tales Publishing, 2011.

Erin Fristad: "A Visit Home," *Moving Mountain: Art and Ideas from Uncrowded Places* #3, 2009.

Jeannine Hall Gailey: "Advice Left Between the Pages of Grimms'" and "She Decides Not to Look Back," *Unexplained Fevers*, Cork City, Ireland: New Binary Press, March 2013.

William Scott Galasso: "Goldsworthy," *Edgz* #13, Winter/Spring 2007 (online).

Maya Ganesan: "The Art of Knowing," *Apologies to an Apple*, Seattle, Washington: Classic Day Publishing, 2009. "Permanent," Hobble Creek Review 6:1. February/Spring 2012.

Cora Goss-Grubbs: "A Mother's Mantra," *Pontoon #10*, Floating Bridge Press, 2008. "Inversion," *Four and Twenty* 3:1, January 2010 (online).

Shane Guthrie: "If they are looking through my trash," *Snowdrift Sapling: Poetry*, Volume 3, 2012.

Winifred Jaeger: "It Begins to Make Sense When You Hear the Music," *American Recorder* XXXV:1, January 1994.

Donald Kentop: "Bill's Ashes," *On Paper Wings*, Seattle, Washington: Rose Alley Press, 2004.

Jared Leising: "The Beer Ted Kooser Owes Us All," *Poet's Musings*, October 31, 2007 (Hans Ostrum blog, online). "Clock Tower Pantoum," *LocusPoint* Volume 1, September 30, 2011 (online).

Marjorie Manwaring: "Tiger Trick," *Diner* 3:2, Fall 2003. "Ephemeroptera," 5 AM #24, 2006. Also published in *Search for a Velvet-Lined Cape*, Woodstock, New York: Mayapple Press, 2013.

Jack McCarthy: "I Didn't Miss the Robins," *Say Goodnight, Grace Notes: New and Corrected Poems*, Channahon, Illinois: EM Press, 2003. Jack McCarthy died on January 17, 2013 at the age of 73.

Rebecca Meredith: "The Widows," *Intergenerational Delta Blues*, Columbus, Ohio: Pudding House Publications, 2006.

Denise Calvetti Michaels: "Labor Day Weekend Along the Hood Canal," *Wetlands Review*, 2007. "Summer Solstice Riff to America from Point Hudson Jetty," *Crosscurrents*, 2012.

Kevin Mooneyham: "Hungry Ghosts in America," *Vox Populi* Volume 4, 2002. "Small Talk," 4th Street, July/August 2002.

Paul E. Nelson: "American Sentences," www.americansentences.com, 2002–2013. "Letter Thirteen—Plum Stain," *A Time Before Slaughter*, Baltimore, Maryland: Apprentice House, November 2009.

Wendelle Peoples: "Still Day," *Love Laments and Whines*, Everett, Washington: privately published. 2003.

dan raphael: "Alexandria," *Missive*, Issue 1, January 2012. "Increment Weather," *The State I'm In*, Winston, Oregon: Nine Muses Books, 2012.

Susan Rich: "Going," *The Southern Review*, Fall/Winter 2012. "The World to Come," *New England Review*, Fall 2011.

Stephen Roxborough: "when someone says i love you and means it" and "remember when we were all water?," *this wonderful perpetual beautiful*, Seattle, Washington: NeoPoiesis Press, 2012.

Raúl Sánchez: "Dandelion," *All Our Brown-Skinned Angels*, Kingston, Washington: MoonPath Press, May 2012. "Smoke," *Pirene's Fountain* 4:9. April 2011 (online).

Michael Schein: "Exhortation," *The Killer Poet's Guide to Immortality*, Seattle, Washington: Wry Ink Publishing, 2012. "Not Saying the F-Word," *Floating Bridge Review* #2, June 2009.

Martha Silano: "Emergency Comfort Kit," *Prairie Schooner* 84:1, Spring 2010. "Size," *Redactions* #14, Summer 2011.

Annette Spaulding-Convy: "Why She Would Take Off Her Shoes Before Jumping from the Golden Gate Bridge," *In Broken Latin*, Fayetteville, Arkansas: University of Arkansas Press, November 2012.

Heather Stark: "Make Him," *Why Doesn't She Just Leave*, Seattle, Washington: Midpacifik Publishing, 2008.

Ann Teplick: "Ritual," *Jack Straw Writers Anthology* 15:1, Fall 2011. "Songbird," *Drash: A Northwest Mosaic* 4:1, May 2010.

Linda Thompson: "Lantern Floating Ceremony," *The Kerf*, Fall 2007 (the inscription on the statue of Sadako at the Peace Park in Hiroshima, Japan reads, "This is our cry, this is our prayer; bring peace to the world"). "Traveling Home," *Write on the Sound*, Fall 2001.

David Lloyd Whited: "who invented this moonlit land" and "Mrs. Coyote must be authentic at all times," *Olde Man Coyote Goes to Towne*, Winston, Oregon: Nine Muses Books, 2012.

Carolyne Wright: "The Cosmic Scholar," *Christian Science Monitor*, 14 October 1977; also published in *Stealing the Children*, Boise, Idaho: Ahsahta Press, 1978. "Success Bomb #45," *The Cincinnati Review* 6:1, Summer 2009; also published in *Mania Klepto: The Book of Eulene*, Cincinnati, Ohio: Turning Point Books, 2011.

Bill Yake: "Finishing It," *Rattle* 7:1, June 2001. "Praising the Fish," *Samsara Quarterly* #11, 2002 (online).

Maged Zaher: "Here, we do second hand smoking well" and "The muse has the right to know," *Thank You for the Window Office*, Brooklyn, New York: Ugly Duckling Presse, 2012.

Contributors

Made in the USA
Charleston, SC
15 May 2015